WHOOP AN' SHOUT!

Other books by Valerie Bloom

Let Me Touch the Sky
Selected Poems for Children

Fruits

Surprising Joy
a novel

WHOOP AN' SHOUT!

Poems by Valerie Bloom

Illustrated by David Dean

MACMILLAN CHILDREN'S BOOKS

For my parents, Edna and John Wright, and for Kenneth,
Claudette, Lorna, Judith, Janette, Wesley, Everett and Dacia

First published 2003 by Macmillan Children's Books
a division of Macmillan Publishers Limited
20 New Wharf Road, London N1 9RR
Basingstoke and Oxford
www.panmacmillan.com

Associated companies throughout the world

ISBN 0 333 99811 1

A CIP catalogue record for this book is available from
the British Library.

Printed and bound in Great Britain by Mackays of Chatham plc, Kent

Contents

Birth of an Island

The sea heaves,
Waves like titanic serpents
Twist and hiss.
Monstrous contractions
Swell the belly of the ocean.
The waters break with gargantuan roar,
And the newborn emerges,
Fresh-faced, pure, and ready
To take its place in the universe.

Mornin' Sport

Chi-chi bud, oh!
Some o' dem a-halla, some a-bawl!
Chi-chi bud, oh!
Some o' dem a-halla, some a-bawl!

Papa start up de diggin' song,
An' we all join in de chorus,
An' it feel like everybody can hear,
From Kingston right to Porus.

De man dem dig wid pick an' fork,
De woman dem prepare de food,
An' all o' we pickney carry water,
An' go fe collect de firewood.

All across de mountain top,
Yuh can hear pickaxe a ring,
Yuh can hear de cutlass dem choppin'
An' yuh can hear all o' we sing.

Chi-chi bud, oh!
Some o' dem a-halla, some a-bawl!
Chi-chi bud, oh!
Some o' dem a-halla, some a-bawl!

When we done carry water,
We climb plum an' mango tree,
Den we all run down de likkle track
Fe play an swim eena de sea.

When Mama shout out, 'lunch time!'
Yam an' saltfish never tas'e so good,
Wid de likkle hint o' woodsmoke
Givin' flavour to de food.

Den de likkle one dem fall asleep,
Right dere pon de grass,
But we get to go down to de river
Ridin' pon Papa jackass.

Papa get up, put on him hat,
An' call out to de men,
An' yuh can hear de sweet, sweet singin'
Startin' up again.

Chi-chi bud, oh!
Some o' dem a-halla, some a-bawl!
Chi-chi bud, oh!
Some o' dem a-halla, some a-bawl!

We tired when de day done,
But all o' we agree,
If Papa have mornin' sport every day,
Bwoy it would o' really suit we.

Work Experience

I went down to the farm one day,
I desperately needed to earn
Didn't know much about farming
But thought that I could learn.

Feeding a few pigs and sheep
Couldn't be that hard,
The farmer looked me up and down
And then said, 'Right, me lad,

'Have a go milking the cow,
Here, take hold of this bucket,
I want it full of milk,' he said.
'Righto,' I said, and took it.

I'd never milked a cow before,
But I'll try anything as a rule,
I headed for the barn, the farmer said,
'Hey, don't forget the stool.'

That cow looked me up and down,
I think that she could tell
I was not used to milking,
And that cow gave me hell.

We wrestled and we tussled
About an hour or more,
And I was bruised and battered
When I stumbled out that door.

I went to find the farmer,
I found him by the sty,
I said, 'This job is not for me,
I've come to say goodbye.

'But before I leave, please tell me,
And you might think that I'm a fool,
But how on earth do you get that cow
To sit still on that stool?'

Wat Tyler

Wat Tyler was a villein,
A great villein, it was said,
But he met a greater villain
And he kinda lost his head.

Wat Tyler was the leader of a peasants'
rebellion against Richard II in 1381.

A Nonet

Let's write a nonet, my sister said,
Why not a clerihew instead?
A cinquain or quick rondel?
Let's write a villanelle
Or else a sonnet,
But she was set
On nonet,
So this
Is.

A Tenon

The
Tenon's
A nonet
Ascending. A
Staircase of rhythm
And rhyme. The lines don't all
Chime at the ending.   But yet
The tenon's quite like the nonet,
For it ends with a rhyming triplet.

Rondel

A rondel is not hard to write,
It isn't a form that will tax you.
It's something you might like to do
Before you turn out the light
And tuck yourself in for the night.
To begin all you need is a clue.
A rondel is not hard to write,
It isn't a form that will tax you.
Sometime when you're not feeling right,
Perhaps stuck in bed with the flu,
Try penning a rondel or two.
It's bound to fill you with delight.
A rondel is not hard to write,
It isn't a form that will tax you.

Wake Up, Amy

Wake up, Amy chile,
water fe get,
the barrel fe fill an'
we no draw one pan yet,
an' me see de sun
a-come up over de hill,
ah know if I lef'
yuh gwine be sleepin' still
at half past ten,
maybe twelve o'clock,
if yuh don't hurry up,
de school gate gwine lock,
before yuh get dere,
we haffe look firewood,
comb we hair,
give de goat dem food,
tie out de donkey,
sweep de yard,
an' eat breakfast,
I know it hard
fe leave you
nice warm bed,
but work dey fe do,
get up, sleepyhead!

Wake up, wake up, wake up beeny bud
Wake up, beeny soon o' mawnin',
Wake up, wake up, wake up beeny bud
Wake up, beeny soon o' mawnin'.

Waiting

I standing here in dis line,
Waiting for me name to call,
Ah not nervous or anxious, or anything,
Ah not really frighten at all.

It don't bother me that Matthew cryin',
Everybody know him a baby,
And Mary probably have a cold
And dat's why she sniffin' – maybe.

I watch dem goin' in de room,
An' is not because me fraid
Why me knee dem shakin' like dis.
From de time me reach third grade

Me stop act like me a coward,
An, is nutten to worry 'bout,
I only jump because me didn' expect
To hear Howard bawl out.

Is jus' a little injection,
It can't hurt much, ah bet,
One stupid little injection
But it can't be my time yet?

Oh gosh, you know me jus' remember,
I lef' something back home,
I better run quick an' get it,
Tell de nurse that I soon come.

* * *

I not cryin' 'cause of one little jab,
Is not yeye-water pon me face,
Is jus' a little sweatin' I sweatin'
'Cause it so hot in dis place.

A Year of Haikus

Spring

A newborn baby
Cries. Listen, it is the sound
Of winter dying.

Summer

The buzzing of a
Bee. And striped towels lying
Lazy on the beach.

Autumn

Leaf mountains in back
Gardens. Useless barriers
'Gainst approaching cold.

Winter

The hedgerow flaunts its
Diamonds. In winter the
Country goes to town.

Today I'm Not Going to School

Today I'm not going to school,
I feel hot; I've a bit of a cough,
I don't like to skive as a rule,
But I've decided to take the day off.

I feel hot; I've a bit of a cough,
I don't think that I'm seriously ill,
But I've decided to take the day off,
Going to bed with a book and a pill.

I don't think that I'm seriously ill,
The doctor's not to be sent for,
Going to bed with a book and a pill
Should make me feel better, I'm sure.

The doctor's not to be sent for,
Custard, potatoes and suet
Should make me feel better, I'm sure,
But today someone else has to do it.

Custard, potatoes and suet!
(I don't like to skive as a rule)
But *today* someone else has to do it,
Today I'm not going to school.

Assurance

There's no such thing as a ghost, Mum said,
The dead stay dead, you'll find,
So there's no need to be scared of the dark.
Thanks, Mum, that's a wraith off my mind.

To a Bully

You have the brain of a dinosaur,
And the countenance to match,
But you're more like an orang-utan,
The way you grunt and scratch.

You are the kind of person
Who laughs, and everyone cries,
When you bend to sniff a flower
It just curls up and dies.

You've one fault –you're unbearable,
And once you start to speak,
No one is left in any doubt
That you're a first-class geek.

You're so low you could stand upright
Under the belly of a worm,
And your ghastly eating habits
Would make a vulture squirm.

You've got a nice personality though,
For a hyena, that is,
You must be quite ecstatic for
They say ignorance is bliss.

If you left your brain to science,
Science would contest the will,
We need you on this planet
Like a fish needs a nostril.

You're ignorant, boring, pathetic,
And I think you should know,
You're a poor excuse for a human being,
And if you were here, I'd tell you so.

Busy

Can't you see I'm busy?
I'm otherwise occupied,
There's no need to look so
Disbelievingly wide-eyed.

I'm counting all the leaves
On the chestnut tree,
I'm listening to the buzzing
Of the honeybee.

I'm contemplating whether
To have fish and chips for lunch,
And if I should quench my thirst
With lemonade or punch.

I'm watching those two grey squirrels
Playing in the oak,
I'm thinking I could buy something
If I weren't so broke.

I'm feeling the grass tickling
As I lean back against the shed,
And I'm listening to the fascinating
Thoughts inside my head.

I wish that I could help you,
But as you can see,
I can't stop what I'm doing now,
I am much too busy.

The Visitor

Cold fingers clawed the face of earth,
Bold winter strutted round,
Bare branches trembled in the wind,
Their leaves mulching the ground.
Dancing snowflakes chuckled in the
Prancing north-east breeze,
Algid rivers stood still, crippled,
Aged women coughed and wheezed.
Sheep shivered in the snow-bound wasteland,
Steep and icy were the paths,
In the houses, people huddled,
Skin slowly cooking round the hearths.
Then it happened, one clear morning
When the bite of cold was sore,
That there came a gentle knocking
On the weatherman's cottage door.
He got up and shambled out to
See, his heart began to sing,
By the door, a young girl smiling,
'Hi,' she said. 'My name is Spring.'

algid = cold/chilly

The Wind

The wind is an angry lion,
Powerful and strong
All night long,
He roams around the house, tossing his mane,
And lashing his tail against the windowpane.
He swats angrily at the doors
With massive paws,
Stops, lifts his head and roars,
Then charges at the house again.

And when the frightened storm clouds rain
Their startled tears upon the earth
And the stars no longer smile,
But hide behind the clouds awhile,
He prowls round, roaring for all he's worth.

But now the nights are still and warm,
He's lost his strong desire to harm,
And pads about, docile and calm.
Then with a rumble, low and deep,
He'll purr contented, and he'll keep
Close watch over a world asleep.

carnival Queen

Ah run all de way from school,
Me foot dem too happy to walk,
An' by de time me reach home
Me coulda hardly talk.

'We goin' to carnival, Mama,
But this wi' tell yuh better,'
An' me reach inside me pocket
An' show her teacher letter.

Ah could see it all a'ready,
De whole class in de parade,
An' me walkin' right in front,
Queen o' de masquerade.

Ah could see de banner dem flyin'
Ah could hear de crowd a-shout,
An' when dem judge de costume,
Ah could hear me name call out.

Mama read de letter, an'
Me see her shake her head,
An' she didn' look pon me,
She look dung pon de groun' instead.

'Yuh can't go to de carnival,'
She say, an' me heart drop,
'It too late to make a costume, an'
They too expensive in de shop.'

Me beg an' cry an' plead with her,
But Mama still say 'no'.
Me can't believe de carnival
Would come, an' me no go.

Mama busy in de yard,
Hangin' out de clothes fe dry,
Papa busy hammerin'
Down by de ole pigsty.

Granny gone to market,
Won' come back 'til after four,
So ah creep inside de house,
An' ah take time shut de door.

Firs' a run to Mama room
An' borrow her red frock,
De one wid lace an' shiny t'ings,
An' de big bow in de back.

Ah take her shoes, de silver one,
Wid front an' side cut off,
Den ah find her silver necklace
An' her long, black, lacy scarf.

Papa tie, ah find that next,
Den race to Granny room,
Pon de way ah make sure
To collect de coconut broom.

Granny silver earring dem
Feel heavy in me han',
So ah put dem in me pocket,
An' pick up de peacock fan.

When ah reach me bedroom,
Ah start to work quick, quick,
An' de firs' t'ing that ah put on,
Was Granny red lipstick.

Then ah put on de red dress,
Tie de scarf right roun' me head,
An' fe de train, me borrow
De green bedspread off o' de bed.

Ah put on de shoes, earrings, necklace,
Tie de necktie roun' me wais'
An' den a wipe a likkle o' Mama
Perfume pon me face.

Ah hear de back door open,
Ah hear when Mama call,
Ah hear Papa comin' in de house,
Walking through de hall.

Ah hear de front gate creakin',
Granny comin' through de yard,
Ah hear her comin' up de step,
An' slammin' de door hard.

Papa come in firs', an' him
Stop in de doorway,
Him mout' jus' open wide,
Like him didn' know what to say.

Den Mama come stand beside him,
An' she say, 'Gran, quick, come look!
Dere's a likkle girl in here
That jus' come out a picture book!'

When Granny come, she see me,
An' she stare an say, 'My word!
This girl prettier than a picture,
She prettier than a doctor bird!

'Ah wonder whey she come from?
Ah wonder who she is?
Yuh think that somebody send her
To come an' play with Liz?'

Me look all roun' de room,
But was me one in de place,
So who dem talking 'bout?
Me feel de smile drop off me face.

Me look pon Mama, Papa, an' Gran,
Me say, 'Who yuh t'ink this is?
Look closer, Mama an' Papa,
Is me, yuh daughter, Liz!'

Papa say, 'It can't be!'
Mama say, 'Not true!
Fe we daughter Liz could never
Be as beautiful as you.'

Me feel me temper risin',
An' me feel me lip start shake,
But Granny look pon me an' laugh
An' say, 'Fe goodness sake,

'Stop tease de chile. No mind, me dear,
Is joke dem jokin' yah,
Of course we know is yuh,
But, gal, yuh pretty sah!'

'So ah can wear this to de carnival?'
Dem look pon one another,
Mama look pon Gran, Gran wink an' say,
'Well yuh sure yuh wouldn' rather

'Wear this costume ah find in de market?'
She take out something shiny an' green,
It was de pretties' costume ah ever see,
Jus' right fe a carnival queen!

Bright Spark

I've just had the results of my final exam,
Everyone marvels at how bright I am,
Not because my intelligence is showing,
But because of the way my red face is glowing.

Circus

The lion tamer cracks his whip,
The lion does a hop and skip,
Accompanied by the crowd's loud roar
He chases his tail around the floor,
He climbs the stool, sits like a clown,
Another crack, he clambers down,
The short attendant lights the fire,
The lion sees the flames climb higher,
Then with one bound, he's through the rings
And for a moment, his heart sings.

The Lyrebird Sadly Cannot Play a Tune

The lyrebird sadly cannot play a tune,
The crane fly won't carry your load,
Don't try, 'cause you'll never boil water
On top of a fire-bellied toad.

The sea does not really lay sea eggs,
The husky's not especially hoarse,
And you wouldn't get far in the Derby
If you tried to ride a sea horse.

Spider monkeys don't weave webs to catch flies,
And you may try as hard as you wish,
But you will never buy a loaf of bread
With a pocketful of silverfish.

A dragonfly's neither fly nor dragon,
A badger's not known to be bad,
You could spend eternity trying,
But you won't teach an adder to add.

There's no truth in the rumour that lions
Are liars, and cheetahs are cheats,
And not everything written is all that it seems,
For language is full of deceit.

Don't Tell Me!

Don't tell me I can't have sausages
In jelly for my tea,
Don't tell me I can't have afters
Unless I eat the broccoli.

Don't tell me that for breakfast
I can't just have ice cream,
Don't tell me not to wear this dress,
For if you do, I'll scream.

Don't tell me that it's time for bed,
Don't call, 'cause I won't come,
You are just the sister,
So don't think that you're the
mum!

The Chickenlamb

My sister would only eat chicken,
But one day Dad cooked some meat,
She tasted it, then licked her lips,
Said, 'This chicken's good to eat.'

'Actually that's not chicken,' Dad said,
And I thought, Oh boy, my mum
Would never ever have told her that,
But Dad just said, 'It's lamb.'

My sister's jaws stopped working,
She played with her slice of yam,
'What kind of lamb is it?' she asked,
'Is it a chicken lamb?'

My father looked bewildered,
But he soon recovered his wit,
'Sure it's a chickenlamb,' he said,
'Shall I tell you all about it?'

'The chickenlamb,' my father said,
'Is a most unusual beast,
Small enough for just one helping,
And large enough for a small feast.

'It is the most useful animal
You will ever hope to see,
For it lays brown eggs for breakfast,
And gives creamy milk for tea.

'It provides wool for our jumpers,
Feathers for our eiderdown,
It has two horns beside its ears,
And a small comb on its crown.

'It crops the grass with dainty teeth,
It pecks corn with its beak,
And "cluck, cluck, baa, baa, cluck, cluck"
Are the words you'll hear it speak.

'Some chickenlambs are half male,
If you give them a year or two,
You'll see them change from chickenlamb
Into cock-a-doodle-ewe.'

I looked from Dad to my sister,
And I thought, this isn't right,
For she grinned, said, 'Can I have some more?'
But I'd lost my appetite.

HoW MaNy?

The egret and the galing,
The owl and the patoo,
The vulture and the john crow,
Is there anybody who
Can tell me how many birds there are?
Six, five, four, three or two?

(Answer on page 81)

I Heard

I heard a moose play on a trombone
I heard a musician barking for his bone
I heard a dog whistling in a tree
I heard a bird laughing loud with glee
I heard a child buzzing in the air
I heard a bee chanting a long prayer
I heard a priest rumbling underground
I heard an earthquake shouting to his hound
I heard the hunter splashing against the piers
I heard the oceans and oh my aching ears.

The Artist

Carefully he chose the colours,
Laid them in a row,
Reached into his bag for brushes,
Bright as a new rainbow.

Then the artist raised his easel,
Tested the canvas and began,
Mixed his paints in waiting palette,
And like a skilful Spiderman

He spun a wide web of enchantment,
With strokes deft, swift and sure,
A little girl stopped by with measles,
And he painted her a cure.

Then he chose lilac for laughter
And all the church bells rang,
He picked out golden tints for happiness
And heavenly choirs sang.

Further brushstrokes fed a baby,
Dressed a beggar, tended the poor
And for the boy feeling excluded,
He painted an open door.

He took bright scarlet shades and transformed
Hatred into love,
Flicked his brush and flowers blossomed,
Rose, hibiscus and foxglove.

Shy recluses, at his bidding,
Came out of their shells,
Prisoners filled the towns with laughter
Set free from their cells.

Then he was gone, though none saw him go,
And folk still remember with a sigh
How the world changed for the better,
On the day that he stopped by.

Terse Verse

ALFRED NOYES

The Highwayman

Robber woos girl, tells her wait,
He'll be back before too late,
Overheard by stable hand,
Who squeals to king's red-coated band,
Girl warns robber with one shot,
He hightails it at fast trot,
Hears of girl's death, comes back mad,
Killed like dog, the silly lad.

ROBERT BROWNING

The Pied Piper of Hamelin

Town infested, fearsome rats
Spoiling ale in council vats,
Piper hired, drives rats away,
Stingy council will not pay,
Lack of guilders has piper stung,
Goes piping off, with Hamelin's young.

Percy Bysshe Shelley

Ozymandias

Empty boast, statue shattered,
King of Kings? Just mortar scattered.

I saw a camel

I saw a camel with five humps
Reclining on a swing,
I saw an eagle with the mumps
Soar skywards on one wing.

I heard an elephant-bird roar
Like a wounded lion,
I heard the hippo-kitten snore
Like steam from a hot iron.

I smelt the thistle and the gorse,
I smelt the flowering heather,
I had to hold my nose because
They smelt like burning leather.

I tasted roasted rhino horns
Like nectar on my tongue,
I tasted a ladder in the yard
And ate it rung by rung.

I touched a blazing log and winced,
For it was cold as sleet,
I stepped on broken glass, it felt
Like mud beneath my feet.

My mother said it wasn't right,
And now I understand her,
Eating big meals late at night
Will set your brain on fire.

I Speak With a Scrape

I speak with a scrape
Followed by a serpent's hiss,
I'm found in the poorest home,
But also in a palace.
My name suggests we're equal,
But that's not strictly true,
For though you're wary of me,
I'm useless without you.
When I'm feeling strongest
You may kill me with one breath,
I was made for one thing only,
To serve you with my death.
Strike me and I'll answer you,
But I'll speak only once,
No matter how often you strike again,
You won't get a response.
I can guide your footsteps,
I can keep you warm,
And if you're careful with me,
I will not do you harm.

What am I?

(Answer on page 81)

SpiderWebs

Naked branches in winter
Spiderwebs catching
Small white flies.

Seafood's Off

Once I ate a starfish,
It tasted worse than tripe,
It gave me indigestion,
Bellyache and gripe.

Another time I thought that I
Would try a small sea snake,
My face and hands broke out in spots,
My skin began to flake.

'Have some pufferfish,' they said,
'You'll love it.' I almost died,
It contracted my skin all over,
And expanded my inside.

I went to a well-known restaurant
And tried their basking shark,
I've recovered from the operation,
But you can still see the mark.

I've had sea urchin, barracuda,
Sea horse, stingray and whale,
And I count myself real lucky
That I've lived to tell the tale.

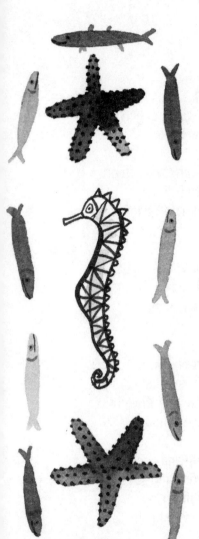

I've told you this at least four times,
You know my history,
So how could you be so thoughtless
To cook me fish for tea?

Igloo

Here is a house like no other,
Open to sun, rain and air,
Well guarded by sharded-glass soldiers,
Enter this house if you dare.

Don't be fooled, it may seem to be empty,
But look carefully and you will see
That the house is not, at second glance,
What it appears to be.

Walk gingerly through the lane of light,
Step soft on the marble floor,
You'll feel your troubles slip away
As you gaze around in awe.

For the house revolves around you,
Each slab has your welfare in mind,
It senses desires, it feels all your thoughts,
Are you lonely? Here you will find

Companionship, friendship and deep love,
Are you suffering from stress and strain?
Are you hurting? Here in this igloo
You'll be free from sickness and pain.

When you're hungry the house will feed you,
When you're hoping for riches and fame
The house knows what you are longing for,
It knows you by your name.

It opens the world so you can see
With the new eyes it's given you,
There are no walls, no doors, no windows,
Nothing obstructing your view.

As you linger, your mind will fill with its light,
Your thoughts become clear as a sunbeam.
Startled, you'll gasp as you realize
That you're no longer the person you seem.

But be warned, just remember, this igloo
Senses joy as well as despair,
Now you know of its power to change you,
Come enter the house, but beware.

Greeting

Sunbeam caresses,
The giddy dewdrop sparkles
At the traitor's kiss.

Rondelet

A summer's day
The chill of winter now is gone,
A summer's day
And traffic clogs the motorway,
The world is heading for Brighton
Folks walk about with nothing on
A summer's day.

Showers

Early May morning,
Rain striding down from the hills,
Arresting the sun.

Nursery Rhyme

Here's a little caterpillar
Crawling up a tree,
Here's a little chicken,
Hungry as can be,
'Hello, little caterpillar,
Come down and play with me.'

'Get lost, d'you think I was born yesterday?'

Omen

From the
Deep silences of
The night, an owl, hunting,
Screams. My heart leaps in fright, and then
Is still.

Newsflash

And now, in news that's just come in,
A fascinating story
That life exists outside the box,
This has caused quite a furore.

Rumour has it that TV
Is not all that it seems,
Not the centre of the universe,
Nor the answer to man's dreams.

An eyewitness was able to verify
That a Mrs Jones from Maldon,
When she sits down to eat with her family,
Will not have the television on.

This reporter has found people who
Actually speak to one another,
Not just in grunts to ask for food,
They converse – hear this – for pleasure.

Unlike us, they do not depend
On TV for recreation,
Amazingly they don't even spend
Much time at a PlayStation.

They masquerade as normal folk,
But one can see through their disguise,
It's said they have no dark circles,
Or bags, beneath their eyes.

We apologize if you find this distressing
But we thought it only right,
To bring this outrage to the public's notice,
Stand by for the weather, goodnight.

Pussycat Up on the Roof

Pussycat up on the roof,
Calling to your kith and kin,
I can tell by your plaintive miaows,
What an excellent mood you're in.

Every night you serenade us,
With your kitty songs of love,
If you want to see tomorrow,
Pussycat, you'd better move.

Outdooring

(This poem was commissioned by the BBC for National Poetry Day, 2002)

Done baby, done cry, yuh madda gone a fountain
Done baby, done cry, yuh madda gone a fountain

Listen to the drums, child, hear what they say,
There's going to be a celebration here today,

The dancers are going to leap through the air,
You grandfather going jump like a young ram from his chair,

The smell of ackee, rice and peas,
Fried chicken and plantain going sweeten the breeze.

We will touch you with cola nut, ginger, sugar and oil,
To help you taste the world, me child.

So hush, me baby, no need to cry,
Let me wipe the eye-water from out of you eye.

Sweetie water never dry, yuh get i' dung a fountain
Sweetie water never dry, yuh get i' dung a fountain

Big Bang

They tell me that a big, big bang,
Bring order to the worl' an' space,
So how come when I make a bang,
Is complete chaos 'bout the place?

Winter

(By the pessimist)

Winter is here, it's time for the frost,
For thick lumpy coats, regardless of cost,
It's time for the snow to stifle the hills,
Time for icicles and huge heating bills,
Time for old bones to start creaking with cold,
For walls covered with damp and papered with mould,
It's time for thunder, lightning and hail,
Time for dark skins to start looking pale,
Time for pink noses to turn purple-blue,
For loud carol singers and their hullabaloo,
Time for the council to pour salt on the street,
To rot your shoe leather and pickle your feet,
For the louring clouds to blot out the sky,
For contentment and comfort to bid you goodbye,
For sensible folk to impersonate
The bear and the badger, and just hibernate.

A Mosquito

A mosquito which tasted a drop of blood
Centuries ago, thought, 'This is good!'
And that is why my cousin Jean
Has blood that's now ten parts quinine.

First contact

The thick hair caressed her back
As she lifted her head,
And stared.

She reached her hand,
Annatto-stained, to the shoulder
Of her small dumb dog.

The parrots, for once,
Were silent,
Breaking off their bickering
To stare with her

Across the blue stillness,
To the three squares of white
Skirting the horizon.

She watched them race closer,
Big-bellied with the wind,
Saw the elaborate canoes beneath.

They were like nothing she had seen before,
So she dropped her digging stick,
And ran.

The Whooping Boys

Whoop, whoop! Whoop, whoop! Whoop, whoop!

Long ago, each October, the hillsides rang
With the unmistakable, haunting song
Of the whooping boys, driving the cattle
Through the fields of pimento, mahoe and wattle,
Past the cane fields to the holding pens
Where the cows would stay until December, when
They would be taken from the byres
To shouts and smell of smouldering fires.

Whoop, whoop! Whoop, whoop! Whoop, whoop!

The flames from those fires have now been doused,
And the byres are empty, which once housed
The herds that supplied the plantation with meat,
Now the only sound in the hills is the beat
Of the woodpecker's beak on breadfruit bark.
Then when the sun is just a spark
In the darkening October sky,
There'll be heard a sound like the north wind's sigh.

Whoop, whoop! Whoop, whoop! Whoop, whoop!

When dusk is a soft blanket over the land,
And the moon is brandishing her silver wand,
The curtains are drawn and the children fed,
Chickens are roosting, babies put to bed,
Then the air will tremble with the familiar sound
Of hundreds of hoof beats pounding the ground,
And the tree-tops will echo with the long, low cry,
For the whooping boys are passing by.

Whoop, whoop! Whoop, whoop! Whoop, whoop!

mahoe = a small tropical tree

Computer Virus

I've got a dangerous virus,
I caught it from a mouse,
I've caught a deadly virus
And it's spreading through my house.

My files are being corrupted,
Business is going bust,
I'd ask for help by email
But I don't know whom to trust.

My memory's been infected,
It's rotten to the core,
I know I should take this computer back
To the electronics store.

For it's a major problem,
Keeps me awake at night,
It was three o'clock this morning
When I turned out the light.

I've been entangled in the Web,
I'm caught fast in the Net,
There's bound to be an escape route,
But I haven't found it yet.

It's making me bad-tempered,
I frown and snap and snarl,
It's driving me to distraction,
And my family up the wall.

Each day I think I've cracked it,
This bug won't bother me any more,
Yet here I am tonight again,
Playing computer games till four.

Rain

She makes the trees sway with delight.
She tells the long grass, 'shiver'.
She puts the laughter in the stream,
And the gurgle in the river.

She drives the thunder grumbling off,
Orders the wind to sing,
Snuffs the lightning's fire out,
Takes the roof tap-dancing.

She pours a drink for the thirsty earth,
Washes the face of the sky,
Puts a sparkle on the leaves
And a glint in the ocean's eye.

She plays a tattoo on the windowpanes,
Paints doors a darker brown,
And creates a brand-new swimming pool
In the centre of the town.

In anger, she will pound the ground
With the force of a cannonball,
But happy, she sings a lullaby,
This celestial waterfall.

Hallowe'en

Ghosts and goblins, ghouls and gremlins
Here on holiday,
Ghosts and goblins, ghouls and gremlins
Coming out to play.

Bats and bogeymen, boggarts, banshees,
Baying at the moon,
Bats and bogeymen, boggarts, banshees,
Bringing misfortune.

Witches, werewolves, warlocks, werecats,
On the prowl tonight,
Witches, werewolves, warlocks, werecats,
Avoiding the lamplight.

But there's no need to close the windows,
No need to bar the door,
It's just the children out at play,
I think – I'm almost sure.

My Dog Was a Bloodhound

My dog was a bloodhound,
He was till yesterday,
That's when he saw the cat
Coming out of the alleyway.

My dog chased the cat,
He chased it in the fog,
He didn't see the brick wall,
Now my bloodhound's a bulldog.

Playing

Jannette is Miss Dadath,
Audrey is Miss Pinns,
My name is Mrs Virgie
(I'm the one who's got the twins).

Joy's baby's name is Bunjie,
And Miss Lucie (that's Claudette)
Should have taken him to the doctor,
But she took him to the vet.

We're making pies till they return,
And our hands are full of mud,
The leaf-soup is almost ready,
Monty says it tastes quite good.

When they're back we'll have a wedding,
So Bonnie is making wreaths,
He'll marry Joy (Miss Davis)
And we've laid out all the seats.

Dacia (who's called Sally)
Will be the one bridesmaid,
Everett will be the parson,
He says he should be paid.

We're just heading for the church
(The shed by Miss Dor's small shop),
When Mama calls out, 'Dinner!'
And the playing has to stop.

There's ackee and salt fish on the table,
And before you can count to ten,
Miss Dadath and Co. are nine siblings
In an ordinary family again.

The Moon is a starfish

The moon is a starfish
Swimming in the sky,
It reaches bright tentacles
Across the earth
To feed on pockets of darkness.

Answers to Riddles

Page 38
How many birds?
Three (The second names are Jamaican for the first)

Page 46
What am I?
A match

Glossary

a-bawl	is/are bawling	**likkle**	little
ah	I		
a-halla	is/are hollering	**mawnin'**	morning
an'	and	**me**	my
		mout'	mouth
'bout	about		
bud	bird	**nutten**	nothing
bwoy	boy		
		o'	of
chile	child	**ole**	old
coulda	could		
		pickney	child
dat	that	**pon**	on/upon
de	the		
dem	them	**roun'**	round
den	then		
dere	there	**sah**	sir
dey	there		
dis	this	**take time**	careful/carefully
dung	down	**tas'e**	taste
		t'ing	thing
eena	in	**t'ink**	think
fe	to/for	**wais'**	waist
firs'	first	**we**	our/we
		whey	where
gal	girl	**wi'**	will
groun'	ground	**wid**	with
gwine	going	**won'**	won't
haffe	have to	**yah**	(do) you hear
han'	hand	**yeye-water**	tears
		yuh	you
jus'	just		

Index of First Lines